LITTLE-FOLK LYRICS

M. Cowles.

Lullaby

LITTLE – FOLK LYRICS BY FRANK DEMPSTER SHERMAN WITH ILLUSTRATIONS BY MAUDE & GENEVIEVE COWLES

Granger Index Reprint Series

BOOKS FOR LIBRARIES PRESS
FREEPORT, NEW YORK

First Published 1897
Reprinted 1969

TO
LITTLE DEMPSTER

STANDARD BOOK NUMBER:
8369-6062-9

LIBRARY OF CONGRESS CATALOG CARD NUMBER:
79-84353

CONTENTS

CONTENTS

x

CONTENTS

LIST OF ILLUSTRATIONS

TO THE LITTLE READERS

WHEN I was young, and long before
The Muse came tapping at my door,
What curious things I used to dream!
How very true they all did seem!
And when I went to bed at night
I begged my mother to recite
The *Tales of Once-upon-a-Time*,
All written down in simple rhyme.
How eagerly I listened, and
How far I went in Fairy-land!
And these same songs she sang to me
Still murmur in my memory.
For me she made the world anew, —
A jewel of each drop of dew;
The autumn leaves of golden tint
Were coins come freshly from the mint;
The birds were poets all, who sang;
The flowers were bells the fairies rang;
And everything I saw became
Another, with another name.

So, little folk, these verses from
The rosary of childhood come
For you to string on Fancy's line,
To be your joy as they were mine, —
To be your joy, and so to bless
Your hearts with song and happiness!

BLOSSOMS

Out of my window I could see
But yesterday, upon the tree,
The blossoms white, like tufts of snow
That had forgotten when to go.

And while I looked out at them, they
Seemed like small butterflies at play,
For in the breeze their flutterings
Made me imagine them with wings.

I must have fancied well, for now
There's not a blossom on the bough,
And out of doors 't is raining fast,
And gusts of wind are whistling past.

With butterflies 't is etiquette
To keep their wings from getting wet,
So, when they knew the storm was near,
They thought it best to disappear.

ANEMONE

A SCULPTOR is the Sun, I know,
Whose shining marble is the snow :
All through the winter, day by day,
He with his golden chisel-ray
Toils patiently that he may bring
A statue forth to honor Spring ;
And when she comes, behold it there, —
A blossom in the gentle air, —
A form of gracious symmetry, —
A fragile white anemone !

DAISIES

At evening when I go to bed
I see the stars shine overhead;
They are the little daisies white
That dot the meadow of the Night.

And often while I'm dreaming so,
Across the sky the Moon will go;
It is a lady, sweet and fair,
Who comes to gather daisies there.

For, when at morning I arise,
There's not a star left in the skies;
She's picked them all and dropped
      them down
Into the meadows of the town.

SPRING'S COMING

The woodland brooks that murmur as they
        go
    In silver ripples through the fringing
        grass
Are harp-strings touched by God : the
    winds that blow
    Are Spring's gay children, singing as
        they pass.

And where the sod is trodden by their feet,
    The Earth, all gladdened by youth's
        warmer blood,
Puts forth her fragile urns of odors
        sweet —
    The violet and fragrant crocus bud.

GOLDEN-ROD

SPRING is the morning of the year,
　　And summer is the noontide bright;
The autumn is the evening clear
　　That comes before the winter's night.

And in the evening, everywhere
　　Along the roadside, up and down,
I see the golden torches flare
　　Like lighted street-lamps in the town.

I think the butterfly and bee,
　　From distant meadows coming back,
Are quite contented when they see
　　These lamps along the homeward track.

But those who stay too late get lost;
　　For when the darkness falls about,
Down every lighted street the Frost
　　Will go and put the torches out!

JANUARY

January, bleak and drear,
First arrival of the year,
Named for Janus, — Janus who,
Fable says, has faces two;
Pray, is that the reason why
Yours is such a fickle sky?
First you smile, and to us bring
Dreams of the returning spring;
Then, without a sign, you frown,
And the snowflakes hurry down,
Making all the landscape white,
Just as if it blanched with fright.
You obey no word or law;
Now you freeze, and then you thaw,
Teasing all the brooks that run
With the hope of constant sun,
Chaining all their feet at last
Firm in icy fetters fast.
Month of all months most contrary,
Sweet and bitter January!

FEBRUARY

FEBRUARY, — fortnights two, —
Briefest of the months are you,
Of the winter's children last.
Why do you go by so fast?
Is it not a little strange
Once in four years you should change,
That the sun should shine and give
You another day to live?
May be this is only done
Since you are the smallest one;
So I make the shortest rhyme
For you, as befits your time:
You 're the baby of the year,
And to me you 're very dear,
Just because you bring the line,
" *Will you be my Valentine?* "

MARCH

MARCH! and all the winds cry, March!
As they sweep the heavens' arch,
Polishing the stars that gem
Earth's resplendent diadem,
Setting all the waters free
From the winter's chancery,
Sending down an avalanche
From the tree's snow-covered branch.
March makes clear the frosty track
That the birds may hasten back
On their northward flight and bring
Jocund carols for the Spring.
March is merry, March is mad,
March is gay, and March is sad ;
Every humor we may know
If we list the winds that blow.
Have you heard the bugle-call
Gathering the soldiers all ?
March is Spring's own trumpeter,
Hailing us to welcome her.

APRIL

OUTDOORS the white rain coming down
Made rivers of the streets in town,
And where the snow in patches lay
It washed the Winter's signs away.
How fast it fell! How warm it felt!
The icicles began to melt:
A silver needle seemed each one
Thrust in the furnace of the Sun —
The Vulcan Sun who forged them all,
In raindrops, crystals round and small.
The air was filled with tiny ropes
On which were strung these April hopes, —
White water-beads that searched the
    ground
Until the thirsty seeds were found.
Then came blue sky; the streets were
    clean,
And in the garden spots of green
Were glistening in golden light, —
The grass — and Spring — almost in sight!
A bluebird sang its song near by;

Oh ! happy Spring *is* come, thought **I** ;
When all at once the air grew chill,
Again the snow-flakes fell until
The ground was covered, and the trees
Stood in the drifts up to their knees.

I think this bird who dared to sing
Was premature about the Spring,
Or else he joked in manner cool,
And caroled lightly, " *April Fool !* "

MAY shall make the world anew;
Golden sun and silver dew,
Money minted in the sky,
Shall the earth's new garments buy.
May shall make the orchards bloom;
And the blossoms' fine perfume
Shall set all the honey-bees
Murmuring among the trees.
May shall make the bud appear
Like a jewel, crystal clear,
'Mid the leaves upon the limb
Where the robin lilts his hymn.
May shall make the wild-flowers tell
Where the shining snowflakes fell,
Just as though each snowflake's heart,
By some secret, magic art,
Were transmuted to a flower
In the sunlight and the shower.
Is there such another, pray,
Wonder-making month as May?

JUNE

O June! delicious month of June,
When winds and birds all sing in tune;
When in the meadows swarm the bees
And hum their drowsy melodies;
O June! the month of bluest skies,
Dear to the pilgrim butterflies,
Who seem gay-colored leaves astray,
Blown down the amber tides of day;
O June! the month of merry song,
Of shadow brief, of sunshine long;
All things on earth love you the best, —
The bird who carols near his nest;
The wind that wakes, and, singing, blows
The spicy perfume of the rose;
And bee, who sounds his muffled horn
To celebrate the dewy morn;
And even all the stars above
At night are happier for love,
As if the mellow notes of mirth
Were wafted to them from the earth.
O June! such music haunts your name,
With you the summer's chorus came.

JULY

JULY, for you the songs are sung
By birds the leafy trees among ;
With merry carolings they wake
The meadows at the morning's break,
And through the day the lisping breeze
Is woven with their tree-top glees :
For you the prattling, pebbly brooks
Are full of tales like story-books :
For you a fragrant incense burns
Within the garden's blossom urns,
Which tempts the bees to hasten home
With honey for their honeycomb.
The river, like a looking-glass,
Reflects the fleecy clouds that pass,
Until it makes us almost doubt
If earth and sky are n't changed about.
July, for you, in silence deep,
The world seems fallen fast asleep,
Save on one glorious holiday,
When all our books we put away,
And every little maid and man
Is proud to be American.

AUGUST

August, month when Summer lies
Sleeping under sapphire skies.
Open all the windows wide,
Drink the orchard's fragrant tide, —
Breath of grass at morning mown
Through the leafy vistas blown ;
Hear the swishing of the scythe,
Sound mellifluent and blithe :
August, month when everywhere
Music floats upon the air
From the harp of minstrel gales,
Playing down the hills and dales :
August, month when sleepy cows
Seek the shade of spreading boughs,
Where the birds alight to sing
And the fruit hangs ripening :
August, month of twilights, when
Day half goes, and comes again ;
August days are guards who keep
Watch while Summer lies asleep.

SEPTEMBER

HERE 's a lyric for September,
Best of all months to remember;
Month when summer breezes tell
What has happened wood and dell,
Of the joy the year has brought,
And the changes she has wrought.
She has turned the verdure red ;
In the blue sky overhead,
She the harvest moon has hung,
Like a silver boat among
Shoals of stars, — bright jewels set
In the earth's blue coronet ;
She has brought the orchard's fruit
To repay the robin's flute
Which has gladdened half the year
With a music, liquid clear ;
And she makes the meadow grass
Catch the sunbeams as they pass,
Till the autumn's floor is rolled
With a fragrant cloth of gold.

OCTOBER

OCTOBER is the month that seems
All woven with midsummer dreams;
She brings for us the golden days
That fill the air with smoky haze;
She brings for us the lisping breeze,
And wakes the gossips in the trees,
Who whisper near the vacant nest
Forsaken by its feathered guest.
Now half the birds forget to sing,
And half of them have taken wing,
Before their pathway shall be lost
Beneath the gossamer of frost.
Now one by one the gay leaves fly
Zigzag across the yellow sky;
They rustle here and flutter there,
Until the bough hangs chill and bare.
What joy for us — what happiness
Shall cheer the day, the night shall
    bless?
'T is Hallowe'en, the very last
Shall keep for us remembrance fast,
When every child shall duck the head
To find the precious pippin red.

M. Cowles.

NOVEMBER

WHO shall sing to bleak November,
Month of frost and glowing ember?
Is there nothing then to praise
In these thirty chilly days?
Ah, but who shall lack for song
When the nights are still and long;
When beside the logwood fire
We may hear the wood-elves' choir,
Making dainty music float
Up the big, brick chimney's throat;
When within the flames and smoke
We may see the fairy folk,
Coming hither, going thither,
Vanishing, we know not whither, —
Or, perhaps they all depart
To the forest's frozen heart,
There to tell the barren trees
Of the fireside's mysteries, —
How they saw some other elves
Just as funny as themselves!

DECEMBER

DECEMBER 's come, and with her brought
A world in whitest marble wrought;
The trees and fence and all the posts
Stand motionless and white as ghosts,
And all the paths we used to know
Are hidden in the drifts of snow.
December brings the longest night,
And cheats the day of half its light.
No song-bird breaks the perfect hush;
No meadow-brook with liquid gush
Runs telling tales in babbling rhyme
Of liberty and summer time,
But frozen in its icy cell
Awaits the sun to break the spell.
Breathe once upon the window glass,
And see the mimic mists that pass, —
Fantastic shapes that go and come
Forever silvery and dumb.

December Santa Claus shall bring, —
Of happy children happy king, —

Who with his sleigh and reindeer stops
At all good people's chimney tops.

Then let the holly red be hung,
And all the sweetest carols sung,
While we with joy remember them —
The journeyers to Bethlehem,
Who followed, trusting from afar
The guidance of that happy star
Which marked the spot where Christ was
        born
Long years ago, one Christmas morn!

KING BELL

LONG years ago there lived a King,
   A mighty man and bold,
Who had two sons, named Dong and Ding,
   Of whom this tale is told.

Prince Ding was clear of voice, and tall,
   A Prince in every line;
Prince Dong, his voice was very small,
   And he but four feet nine.

Now both these sons were very dear
   To Bell, the mighty King.
They always hastened to appear
   When he for them would ring.

Ding never failed the first to be,
   But Dong, he followed well,
And at the second summons he
   Responded to King Bell.

This promptness of each royal Prince
   Is all of them we know,

Except that all their kindred since
 Have done exactly so.

And if you chance to know a King
 Like this one of the song,
Just listen once — and there is Ding ;
 Again — and there is Dong.

IN THE MEADOW

THE meadow is a battle-field
　　Where Summer's army comes,
Each soldier with a clover shield,
　　The honey-bees with drums.
　　　　Boom, rat-ta ! they march, and pass
　　　　　The captain tree who stands
　　　　Saluting with a sword of grass
　　　　　And giving them commands.

'T is only when the breezes blow
　　Across the woody hills,
They shoulder arms, and, to and fro,
　　March in their full-dress drills.
　　　　Boom, rat-ta ! they wheel in line
　　　　　And wave their gleaming spears ;
　　　"Charge!" cries the captain, giving
　　　　　sign,
　　　　　And every soldier cheers.

But when the day is growing dim
　　They gather in their camps

And sing a good thanksgiving hymn
  Around the firefly lamps.
    Rat-tat-ta ! the bugle-notes
      Call " good-night " to the sky :
    I hope they all have overcoats
      To keep them warm and dry.

FAIRY JEWELS

O WHITE moon sailing down the sky,
I watch you when in bed I lie;
I watch you on the calm, blue deep,
And dream of you when fast asleep.
I fancy as I see you float
That you are some good fairy's boat,
And winds that in my windows blow
Are the same winds that make you go;
Each star that shines for me so bright
For you is just a beacon light.
I half believe that it is you
Who bring to us the morning dew, —
Each drop is so much like a gem,
I think the fairy gathers them,
And leaning over as you pass
Lets millions fall upon the grass.

In winter, when the wind I hear
I know the clouds will disappear;
For 't is the wind who sweeps the sky
And piles the snow in ridges high.

In spring, when stirs the wind, I know
That soon the crocus buds will show;
For 't is the wind who bids them wake
And into pretty blossoms break.

In summer when it softly blows,
Soon red I know will be the rose,
For 't is the wind to her who speaks,
And brings the blushes to her cheeks.

In autumn, when the wind is up,
I know the acorn 's out its cup;
For 't is the wind who takes it out,
And plants an oak somewhere about.

HUMMING–BIRD SONG

Humming-bird,
Not a word
　Do you say ;
Has your throat
No sweet note
　To repay
Honey debts
It begets
　When you go
On the wing
Pilfering
　To and fro ?

May be you
Whisper to
　Bloom and leaf
On the vine
Secrets fine
　In your brief
Calls on them,

Wingèd gem.
Not a word
You reply!
Off you fly,
Humming-bird!

PEBBLES

OUT of a pellucid brook
Pebbles round and smooth I took:
Like a jewel, every one
Caught a color from the sun, —
Ruby red and sapphire blue,
Emerald and onyx too,
Diamond and amethyst, —
Not a precious stone I missed:
Gems I held from every land
In the hollow of my hand.
Workman Water these had made;
Patiently through sun and shade,
With the ripples of the rill
He had polished them until,
Smooth, symmetrical and bright,
Each one sparkling in the light
Showed within its burning heart
All the lapidary's art;
And the brook seemed thus to sing:
Patience conquers everything!

IN THE ORCHARD

O ROBIN in the cherry-tree,
I hear you caroling your glee.
The platform where you lightly tread
Is lighted up with cherries red,
And there you sing among the boughs,
Like Patti at the opera-house.

Who is the hero in your play
To whom you sing in such a way?
And why are you so gayly dressed,
With scarlet ribbons on your breast?
And is your lover good and true?
And does he always sing to you?

Your orchestra are winds that blow
Their blossom notes to me below,
And all the trembling leaves are throngs
Of people clapping for your songs.
I wonder if you like it when
I clap for you to sing again.

In the Or-chard

M. Cowles.

O Robin in the cherry
- tree,
I hear you
caroling
your glee,
The platform
where you
lightly tread
is lighted up
with cherries red,
And there you sing among the boughs,
Like Patti at the opera-house.

A REAL SANTA CLAUS

Santa Claus, I hang for you,
By the mantel, stockings two:
One for me and one to go
To another boy I know.

There 's a chimney in the town
You have never traveled down.
Should you chance to enter there
You would find a room all bare:
Not a stocking could you spy,
Matters not how you might try;
And the shoes, you 'd find are such
As no boy would care for much.
In a broken bed you 'd see
Some one just about like me,
Dreaming of the pretty toys
Which you bring to other boys,
And to him a Christmas seems
Merry only in his dreams.

All he dreams then, Santa Claus,
Stuff the stocking with, because
When it 's filled up to the brim
I 'll be Santa Claus to him !

CHERRIES

APRIL brought the blossoms out,
May winds scattered them about,
Till the grassy floor below
Whitened with their fragrant snow;
Then came June with golden sun,
Of all months the fairest one,
Smiling on the trees and brooks
Like a child with picture-books.

In the green leaves overhead
Little lights were burning red;
Looking up, it seemed that I
Saw the stars in fairy sky
Glistening the leaves among,
Lanterns by the pixies hung;
But I heard a song-bird pipe
" Cherry ripe! " and " Cherry ripe! "

He who sings of cherries best
Wears their colors on his breast;
He their poet is, and he

Makes his dwelling in their tree.
'T is not strange his song is sweet ;
Think — the cherries he can eat !
Busy with his feathered wits
He makes bare the cherry pits.

Bring the basket, little maid ;
Let us lend Sir Robin aid.
I will climb among the boughs
Where he has his tiny house,
And if I can find him there
I will ask him please to spare
Of his tempting cherry feast
One small basketful at least.

I will tell him how in spring
When you first had heard him sing,
All upon the garden ground
You the bread-crumbs threw around :
Then, if he 's the bird I think,
He will answer in a wink,
" Certainly : I 'd help you pick,
If their stems were not so thick ! "

FLYING KITE

I OFTEN sit and wish that I
Could be a kite up in the sky,
And ride upon the breeze, and go
Whatever way it chanced to blow.
Then I could look beyond the town,
And see the river winding down,
And follow all the ships that sail
Like me before the merry gale,
Until at last with them I came
To some place with a foreign name.

KRISS KRINGLE

AWAY with melancholy!
  This day is for delight;
When mistletoe and holly
  In wreaths and garlands bright
Are hung above the ingle,
And joyous voices mingle
To welcome in Kriss Kringle,
  Who comes clad all in white!

Green spray and crimson berry
  A crown for him shall be;
Gay catch and carol merry
  Shall fill his heart with glee,
Shall match his sleigh-bells' jingle
And warm his ears a-tingle, —
A greeting to Kriss Kringle,
  The Christmas Fairy he!

Within his sleigh he carries
  The presents high up-piled;
Not long with us he tarries,
  By leaf and song beguiled.

God-speed, down dale and dingle,
May there not be a single
Forgotten one, Kriss Kringle ;
But gifts for every child !

WIZARD FROST

WONDROUS things have come to pass
On my square of window-glass.
Looking in it I have seen
Grass no longer painted green,
Trees whose branches never stir,
Skies without a cloud to blur,
Birds below them sailing high,
Church-spires pointing to the sky,
And a funny little town
Where the people, up and down
Streets of silver, to me seem
Like the people in a dream,
Dressed in finest kinds of lace:
'T is a picture, on a space
Scarcely larger than the hand,
Of a tiny Switzerland,
Which the wizard Frost has drawn
'Twixt the nightfall and the dawn.
Quick! and see what he has done
Ere 't is stolen by the Sun.

THE JUGGLER

FROM these downy flakes of snow
  Winter scatters everywhere,
Fragrant violets shall grow
  In the springtime's balmy air.

Every snowdrop on the numb
  Branches of the barren tree
Shall a ruby bud become
  When the warm sun sets it free.

And the icicles that shine
  Dagger-like and crystal-clear
In the fingers of the vine,
  Trembling leaves shall then appear.

We shall know when comes this strange
  Juggler April, who shall bring
Out of snow-drifts, "Presto, change!"
  Birds and blossoms of the spring!

A FAIRY STORY

THIS is what a fairy heard;
    Listening beside a stream, —
    Water talking in its dream.
That is what I call absurd.

This is what the water said:
    When I grow up big, I'll be
    Like the river or the sea.
And the fairy shook her head.

Then she went upon her way
    Far across the hills and vales
    And she heard so many tales
She forgot the dream one day.

But, at last, spread out to view,
    Lay the ocean: then, once more,
    She heard water on the shore
Whisper: *I remember you.*

Once I was a tiny drop
  Dreaming in a meadow-brook.
  I was little then ; but look, —
Now I've grown enough to stop !

THE SHADOWS

All up and down in shadow-town
  The shadow children go ;
In every street you 're sure to meet
  Them running to and fro.

They move around without a sound,
  They play at hide-and-seek,
But no one yet that I have met
  Has ever heard them speak.

Beneath the tree you often see
  Them dancing in and out,
And in the sun there 's always one
  To follow you about.

G. COWLES.

Go where you will, he follows still,
   Or sometimes runs before,
And, home at last, you 'll find him fast
   Beside you at the door.

A faithful friend is he to lend
   His presence everywhere ;
Blow out the light — to bed at night —
   Your shadow-mate is there !

Then he will call the shadows all
   Into your room to leap,
And such a pack ! they make it black,
   And fill your eyes with sleep !

G. COWLES

HIDE-AND-SEEK

Now hide the flowers beneath the snow,
    And Winter shall not find them ;
Their safety nooks he cannot know :
    They left no tracks behind them.

The little brooks keep very still,
    Safe in their ice-homes lying ;
Let Winter seek them where he will,
    There 's no chance for his spying.

Gone are the birds : they 're hiding where
    The Winter never searches ;
Safe in the balmy Southern air,
    They sing on sunlit perches.

But comes the Spring at last to look
    For all her playmates hidden,
And one by one — flower, bird, and
        brook —
    Shall from its place be bidden.

Then shall the world be glad and gay,
    The birds begin their chorus,
The brooks sing, too, along their way,
    And flowers spring up before us!

THE ARCHER

His home is yonder in the sky;
  There, when the chase is o'er,
He hangs his gorgeous bow on high
  Above the open door.

And sitting down he looks around
  The green fields wide and far,
Where prostrate lying on the ground
  His many victims are.

Strong is his arm, he knows it well,
  And sure his steady aim;
For him the missing arrows tell
  The number of the game.

Come out, come out! the hunt is done;
  No danger shall we know;
For yonder see beneath the sun
  His promise and his bow!

A FUNNY FELLOW

THERE is a funny fellow
　Who goes by every day :
When sad, his voice is mellow,
　But shrill when he is gay.

Despite of my endeavor
　To see him, though we 've met
I must confess I never
　Have seen his features yet.

I know he pulls the thistles
　That grow along the lane,
And pricks himself, and whistles
　To drive away the pain.

And when the snow is falling
　So fast I may not see,
I often hear him calling
　Across the fields to me.

He certainly is funny,
　For, when I can go out,

If it is warm and sunny
   He seldom is about.

He sings to me, and makes me
   A sleepy child at night ;
He sings again, and wakes me,
   At early morning bright.

SPINNING TOP

WHEN I spin round without a stop
And keep my balance like the top,
I find that soon the floor will swim
Before my eyes; and then, like him,
I lie all dizzy on the floor
Until I feel like spinning more.

SMILES AND TEARS

I SMILE, and then the Sun comes out;
He hides away whene'er I pout;
He seems a very funny sun
To do whatever he sees done.

And when it rains he disappears;
Like me, he can't see through the tears.
Now is n't that the reason why
I ought to smile and never cry?

In more than this is he like me;
For every evening after tea
He closes up his eyelids tight,
And opens them at morning's light.

THE CANARY

Up in your cage of gold,
    Singing us all awake,
What, if it might be told,
    What is the wish you 'd make?

Is it, " I 'd like to be
    Out in the open air,
Out of this cage, and free,
    Free to go anywhere?"

You 're such a happy bird,
    Caroling all day long,
Nobody ever heard
    You sing a solemn song.

So I have come to think
    This is your carol sweet:
" Plenty have I to drink,
    Plenty have I to eat;

" So I 'm content to stay
    Here in my golden ring,
Nothing to do all day,
    Only to eat and sing."

CLOUDS

THE sky is full of clouds to-day,
  And idly, to and fro,
Like sheep across the pasture, they
  Across the heavens go.
I hear the wind with merry noise
  Around the housetops sweep,
And dream it is the shepherd boys, —
  They 're driving home their sheep.

The clouds move faster now ; and see!
  The west is red and gold.
Each sheep seems hastening to be
  The first within the fold.
I watch them hurry on until
  The blue is clear and deep,
And dream that far beyond the hill
  The shepherds fold their sheep.

Then in the sky the trembling stars
  Like little flowers shine out,
While Night puts up the shadow bars,
  And darkness falls about.

I hear the shepherd wind's good-night —
"Good-night, and happy sleep!" —
And dream that in the east, all white,
Slumber the clouds, the sheep.

LEAVES AT PLAY

SCAMPER, little leaves, about
    In the autumn sun ;
I can hear the old Wind shout,
    Laughing as you run,
And I have n't any doubt
    That he likes the fun.

When you 've run a month or so,
    Very tired you 'll get ;
But the same old Wind, I know,
    Will be laughing yet
When he tucks you in your snow-
    Downy coverlet.

So, run on and have your play,
    Romp with all your might ;
Dance across the autumn day,
    While the sun is bright.
Soon you 'll hear the old Wind say,
    " Little leaves, Good-night ! "

SHADOW PICTURES

In the day or night,
When the lamps are bright,
　Far up in the sky's blue dome,
Every kind of tree
Is a child like me,
　Amusing himself at home.

On the ground below
In the brilliant glow
　Of stars, or of moon or sun,
There the shadows fall
On the grassy wall,
　And over the garden run.

There are cats and kings,
There are birds with wings,
　And curious kinds of men ;
And they dance and play
In a funny way,
　And vanish, and come again.

Oh, I wish I knew
How their fingers do
   Such tricks with the shadows dark ;
Then I 'd make the birds
And the beasts in herds,
   To go in a shadow ark.

And the flood should come,
As it once did, from
   The lamp on the parlor shelf ;
And my shadow boat
On the wall should float,
   And Noah should be myself.

GHOST FAIRIES

WHEN the open fire is lit,
  In the evening after tea,
Then I like to come and sit
  Where the fire can talk to me.

Fairy stories it can tell,
  Tales of a forgotten race, —
Of the fairy ghosts that dwell
  In the ancient chimney place.

They are quite the strangest folk
  Anybody ever knew,
Shapes of shadow and of smoke
  Living in the chimney flue.

"Once," the fire said, "long ago,
  With the wind they used to rove,
Gipsy fairies, to and fro,
  Camping in the field and grove.

"Hither with the trees they came
  Hidden in the logs ; and here,

GHOST FAIRIES.

WHEN THE OPEN FIRE IS LIT,
IN THE EVENING AFTER TEA,
THEN I LIKE TO COME AND SIT
WHERE THE FIRE CAN TALK
TO ME.
FAIRY STORIES IT CAN TELL,
TALES OF A FORGOTTEN RACE,—
OF THE FAIRY GHOSTS THAT DWELL
IN THE ANCIENT CHIMNEY PLACE.

Hovering above the flame,
  Often some of them appear."

So I watch, and, sure enough,
  I can see the fairies !   Then,
Suddenly there comes a puff —
  Whish ! — and they are gone again !

SONG FOR WINTER

Now winter fills the world with snow,
Wild winds across the country blow,
And all the trees, with branches bare,
Like beggars shiver in the air.
Oh, now hurrah for sleds and skates!
A polar expedition waits
When school is done each day for me —
Off for the ice-bound arctic sea.

The ice is strong upon the creek,
The wind has roses for the cheek,
The snow is knee-deep all around,
And earth with clear blue sky is crowned.
Then come, and we may find the hut
Wherein the Esquimau is shut,
Or see the polar bear whose fur
Makes fun of the thermometer.

Let us who want our muscles tough
Forsake the tippet and the muff.
The keen fresh wind will do no harm,
The leaping blood shall keep us warm,

A spin upon our arctic main
Shall drive the clouds from out the brain,
And for our studies we at night
Shall have a better appetite.

A DEWDROP

LITTLE drop of dew,
　　Like a gem you are;
I believe that you
　　Must have been a star.

When the day is bright,
　　On the grass you lie;
Tell me then, at night
　　Are you in the sky?

JESTER BEE

THE garden is a royal court
　　Whose jester is the bee,
And with his wit and merry sport
　　He fills the place with glee.

He sings love ditties to the Rose
　　Who is the queen of all ;
To princess Lily up he goes
　　And whispers she is tall ;

He pulls prince Pansy by the ear ;
　　He does all sorts of things
That are ridiculous and queer —
　　But all the while he sings.

He does not seem to think it wrong
　　Such liberties to take ;
And they who love his happy song
　　Forgive him for its sake.

And when at last the royal clown
　　Takes off his jester's mask,
He seriously sits him down
　　Before his honey task.

Then to himself he sings away,
　　And here's the burden true :
" Oh, sweet are all my hours of play,
　　And sweet my honey, too ! "

M. A. COWLES.

SNOWFLAKES

Out of the sky they come
   Wandering down the air, —
Some to the roofs and some
   Whiten the branches bare ;

Some in the empty nest,
   Some on the ground below,
Until the world is dressed
   All in a gown of snow.

Dressed in a fleecy gown
   Out of the snowflakes spun ;
Wearing a golden crown, —
   Over her head the sun.

Out of the sky again
   Ghosts of the flowers that died
Visit the earth, and then
   Under the white drifts hide.

DREAMS

Who can tell us whence they come,
What mysterious region from?
In what fairy country lies
That strange city of surprise,
Whither we in slumber go
By a path we do not know?
Is it near or far away?
And the people, who are they?

Once when I was there, the town
Seemed entirely upside down:
Roofs of barns and houses stood
Where the stone foundations should,
And the streets all seemed to run
Straight as arrows to the sun
Where, like ribbons, they were wound
Its great, golden spool around.

All the men and horses there,
Topsy-turvy in the air,
Walked and trotted on the blue
Pavements of the avenue.

But at morning when I woke,
I discovered 't was a joke,
For the first thing I found out
Was that I had turned about.

How to go there, who can tell,
Where these fairy people dwell?
Strange it is that morning's light
Cannot show the path of night;
Stranger yet that we can keep
It so surely in our sleep;
But the very strangest seems
Being wide-awake in dreams.

MAY-CHILDREN

CAPTIVES to winter's cruel king,
    In gloomy dungeons cast
The merry children of the spring
    Lay bound in fetters fast

They heard the wind, their surly guard,
    His angry summons roar,
And trembled when the sleet fell hard
    Against their prison door.

The wild flower whispered to the grass,
    " What hope have we to live ? "
But answer none made he.   Alas!
    He had no hope to give.

So in the darkness sad they wept,
    Nor any comfort won,
Save when into their sleep there crept
    Dreams of the gentle sun.

But once while they were dreaming so,
    Came April's soldier rains,

Who burst their prison bars of snow,
    And freed them of their chains.

Then forth they went into the world,
    Spring's children bright and gay,
And to the fragrant breeze unfurled
    Their banner blooms of May.

ROBIN'S APOLOGY

ONE morning in the garden
I heard the robin's song:
" I really beg your pardon
For tarrying so long ;

" And this is just the reason, —
Whatever way I flew,
I met a backward season,
Which kept me backward too."

SOLDIERS OF THE SUN

ALONG the margin of the world
They march with their bright banners
  furled,
Until, in line of battle drawn,
They reach the boundaries of dawn.
They cross the seas and rivers deep,
They climb the mountains high and steep,
And hurry on until in sight
Of their black enemy, the Night ;
Then madly rush into the fray
The armies of the Night and Day.
Swiftly the shining arrows go ;
The bugling winds their warnings blow.
Strive as he will, the Night is pressed
Farther and farther down the west.
With golden spear and gleaming lance
The cohorts of the Day advance,
Until the victory is won
By his brave Soldiers of the Sun.

SNOW SONG

Over valley, over hill,
Hark, the shepherd piping shrill !
Driving all the white flocks forth
From the far folds of the North.
    Blow, Wind, blow ;
        Weird melodies you play,
    Following your flocks that go
        Across the world to-day.

How they hurry, how they crowd
When they hear the music loud !
Grove and lane and meadow full
Sparkle with their shining wool.
    Blow, Wind, blow
        Until the forests ring :
    Teach the eaves the tunes you know,
        And make the chimney sing !

Hither, thither, up and down
Every highway of the town,
Huddling close, the white flocks all
Gather at the shepherd's call.

SNOW SONG.

OVER VALLEY, OVER HILL,
HARK, THE SHEPHERD
PIPING SHRILL !
DRIVING ALL THE WHITE
FLOCKS FORTH
FROM THE FAR FOLDS OF
THE NORTH.

Blow, Wind, blow
  Upon your pipes of joy ;
All your sheep the flakes of snow
  And you their shepherd boy !

THE RAIN-HARP

WHEN out-of-doors is full of rain,
I look out through the window-pane
And see the branches of the trees
Like people dancing to the breeze.

They bow politely, cross, and meet,
Salute their partners, and retreat,
And never stop to rest until
They reach the end of the quadrille.

I listen, and I hear the sound
Of music floating all around,
And fancy 't is the Breeze who plays
Upon his harp on stormy days.

The strings are made of rain, and when
The branches wish to dance again,
They whisper to the Breeze, and he
Begins another melody.

I 've heard him play the pretty things
Upon those slender, shining strings;
And when he 's done — he 's very sharp —
He always hides away the harp.

ELFIN LAMPS

WHY all the stars in the sky are so bright,
  I am sure no one knows but themselves
    up there.
Are they the lamps which are hung out at
    night
  For the fays and the gnomes and the
    elves up there ?

THE little leaves upon the trees
   Are written o'er with notes and words,
The pretty madrigals and glees
   Sung by the merry minstrel birds.

Their teacher is the Wind, I know ;
   For while they 're busy at their song,
He turns the music quickly so
   The tune may smoothly move along.

So all through summer-time they sing,
   And make the woods and meadows sweet,
And teach the brooks, soft murmuring,
   Their dainty carols to repeat.

And when, at last, their lessons done,
   The winter brings a frosty day,
Their teacher takes them, one by one,
   Their music, too, and goes away.

SHADOW CHILDREN

WHEN the sun shines, then I see
Shadows underneath the tree
Gliding merrily around,
Never making any sound,
Playing at their games, no doubt, —
Games I do not know about.

All day long together so
Lightly o'er the ground they go,
Meet and separate and meet,
Scamper down the shadow street,
For an instant here, and then
Just as quickly gone again.

When with clouds the skies are gray,
In their house the shadows stay,
With their picture-books and toys,
Like all other girls and boys ;
But as soon as shines the sun
Out of doors they gladly run.

So for hours they play, until
Sinks the sun behind the hill;
Then, like me, they go to bed,
In the tree-house overhead,
And the winds their cradles swing
To the lullabies they sing.

FAIRY SHIPWRECK

ONE morning when the rain was done,
  And all the trees adrip,
I found, all shining in the sun,
  A storm-wrecked fairy ship.

Its hull was fashioned of a leaf,
  A tiny twig its mast,
And high upon a green-branch reef
  By winds it had been cast.

A spider's web, the fragile sail,
  Now flying loose and torn,
Once spread itself to catch the gale
  By which the ship was borne.

Its voyages at last were o'er,
  And gone were all the crew ;
And did they safely get ashore ?
  Alas, I wish I knew !

BEES

BEES don't care about the snow;
I can tell you why that's so:

Once I caught a little bee
Who was much too warm for me!

THE WATERFALL

TINKLE, tinkle !
Listen well !
Like a fairy silver bell
In the distance ringing,
Lightly swinging
In the air ;
'T is the water in the dell
Where the elfin minstrels dwell,
Falling in a rainbow sprinkle,
Dropping stars that brightly twinkle,
Bright and fair,
On the darkling pool below,
Making music so ;
'T is the water elves who play
On their lutes of spray.
Tinkle, tinkle !
Like a fairy silver bell ;
Like a pebble in a shell ;
Tinkle, tinkle !
Listen well !

LULLABY

SLUMBER, slumber, little one, now
The bird is asleep in his nest on the bough ;
The bird is asleep, he has folded his wings,
And over him softly the dream-fairy sings :
      Lullaby, lullaby — lullaby !
        Pearls in the deep —
          Stars in the sky,
        Dreams in our sleep ;
          So lullaby !

Slumber, slumber, little one, soon
The fairy will come in the ship of the
    moon :
The fairy will come with the pearls and the
    stars,
And dreams will come singing through
    shadowy bars :
      Lullaby, lullaby — lullaby !
        Pearls in the deep —
          Stars in the sky,
        Dreams in our sleep ;
          So lullaby !

Slumber, slumber, little one, so ;
The stars are the pearls that the dream-
    fairies know,
The stars are the pearls, and the bird in
    the nest,
A dear little fellow the fairies love best :
    Lullaby, lullaby — lullaby !
      Pearls in the deep —
        Stars in the sky,
      Dreams in our sleep ;
        So lullaby !

WINTER'S ACROBATS

By night he spread his white rugs down
Upon the highways of the town;

His posters on the fences told
Of games and pleasures manifold,

And promised every girl and boy
A day of undivided joy,

Of merry sport and healthy fun,
In case there were not any sun.

The gray sky was his spacious tent,
And nearly all the children went.

Some took their sleds, some took their
    skates,
Some took themselves, and some their
    mates.

Then all day long, on pond and hill,
They slid and coasted with a will,

And built snow images and forts,
And played at all their jolly sports.

And when at last 't was time to end
The happy games and homeward wend,

They cried, while tossing high their hats,
"Three cheers for Winter's Acrobats!"

VACATION SONG

WHEN study and school are over,
  How jolly it is to be free,
Away in the fields of clover,
  The honey-sweet haunts of the bee !

Away in the woods to ramble,
  Where, merrily all day long,
The birds in the bush and bramble
  Are filling the summer with song.

Away in the dewy valley
  To follow the murmuring brook,
Or sit on its bank and dally
  Awhile with a line and a hook.

Away from the stir and bustle,
  The noise of the town left behind :
Vacation for sport and muscle,
  The winter for study and mind.

There 's never a need to worry,
  There 's never a lesson to learn,

There's never a bell to hurry,
   There's never a duty to spurn.

So play till the face grows ruddy
   And muscles grow bigger, and then
Go back to the books and study;
   We'll find it as pleasant again.

THE SNOW-BIRD

WHEN all the ground with snow is white,
  The merry snow-bird comes,
And hops about with great delight
  To find the scattered crumbs.

How glad he seems to get to eat
  A piece of cake or bread !
He wears no shoes upon his feet,
  Nor hat upon his head.

But happiest is he, I know,
  Because no cage with bars
Keeps him from walking on the snow
  And printing it with stars.

THE FAIRIES' DANCE

ONCE in the morning when the breeze
    Set all the leaves astir,
And music floated from the trees
    As from a dulcimer,
I saw the roses, one by one,
    Bow gracefully, as though
A fairy dance were just begun
    Upon the ground below.

The lilies white, beside the walk,
    Like ladies fair and tall,
Together joined in whispered talk
    About the fairies' ball ;
The slender grasses waved along
    The garden path, and I
Could almost hear the fairies' song
    When blew the light wind by.

I waited there till noon to hear
    The elfin music sweet ;
I saw the servant bees appear
    In golden jackets neat ;
And though I wished just once to see
    The happy little elves,
They were so much afraid of me
    They never showed themselves !

THE ROSE'S CUP

Down in a garden olden, —
   Just where, I do not know, —
A buttercup all golden
   Chanced near a rose to grow ;
And every morning early,
   Before the birds were up,
A tiny dewdrop pearly
   Fell in this little cup.

This was the drink of water
   The rose had every day ;
But no one yet has caught her
   While drinking in this way.
Surely, it is no treason
   To say she drinks so yet,
For that may be the reason
   Her lips with dew are wet.

THE SNOW-WEAVER

BACK and forth the shuttles go
Fashioning the cloth of snow,
And the weaver you may hear
At the wind-loom singing clear :

"Slumber, little flowers, and dream
Of the silver-throated stream,
Shining through the April day
As it were a music ray
Bearing melody along
From the mellow sun of song.
Slumber, little fragrant faces,
Dreaming in your quiet places ;
Soon the dreams shall pass — and then
You and Spring shall wake again ! "

Thus the weaver at his loom
Sings away the winter's gloom,
While he weaves the coverlet
For the dreamers who forget :

" Slumber, little flowers, and dream
Of the April's golden beam
Which shall come and fill your eyes
With the sunlight of surprise ;
Waking, you shall hear once more
Song-birds at the daybreak's door.
Slumber, little fragrant faces,
Dreaming in your quiet places.
Soon the dreams shall pass — and then
You and Spring shall wake again ! "

THE STORY–TELLER

THEY gather round him, one and all,
A group of happy children small;

Their mouths are open wide; their eyes
Seem almost twice their normal size;

Some stand, some sit, and not a word
From any one of them is heard.

Now all is ready quite, for now
The story-teller rubs his brow,

And questions them : " What shall it be ?
A fairy-tale from memory ?

" Or shall I tell it in a song,
And make up as I go along ?

" Which shall it be, in prose or rhyme,
This tale of once upon a time ?

Or will you have a story true ?
Choose anything that pleases you."

A busy hum goes round, and then
The voices quickly hush again ;

For this small audience knows well
That any story he may tell,

Or any song that he may sing,
Will be a most delightful thing.

" We 'll let you choose," they cry, and so
He tells a tale of long ago.

There 's something told about a gem
Set in a Sultan's diadem,

Which shone in such a brilliant way
It changed the darkness into day.

And there 's a robber and a lot
Of other people in the plot, —

A prince, a princess, and a page,
A parrot in a golden cage.

And there's the palace court-yard where
The Sultan walks when it is fair;

And there's a funny dwarf he had
To cheer him up when he was sad.

Of course the robber comes to grief
The gem was in his handkerchief:

The parrot 't is who picked it up
And dropped it in his water cup;

And then the prince the parrot bought,
And found the gem the Sultan sought.

So runs for one long hour the tale,
And finds the robber safe in jail.

The parrot has become quite tame,
And calls the princess by her name;

The page has had his pay increased,
Which he deserved, to say the least;

The dwarf — the Sultan's merry dwarf —
Has been presented with a scarf,

Whose colors made the Sultan vext,
And that 's
        Continued in the next.

THE RAINBOW

AFTER the rain goes by,
Curving across the sky
Behold the bow of light, —
God's promise shining bright!
Under this glowing arch
The myriad mist-folk march,
And yonder — lo, the Sun!
  Glistens the grass once more,
  The birds sing at the door,
  Blue the sky as before,
     And the rain is done!

Slowly the meadow mist
Melts into amethyst;
Slowly the rainbow fair
Fades in the amber air;
Wakes in the west a breeze
Whispering through the trees
The secrets of the Sun.

Gleams like a gem the rose,
Open its red door blows,
Thither the glad bee goes, —
   And the rain is done!

THE STORY OF OMAR

LONG centuries ago, three Persian boys,
Thinking upon their hopes of future joys,
Between them — Omar, Abdul, and Has-
    sán —
A lasting compact made, and thus it ran :

Abdul and Omar and Hassán.   These
    three,
School-mates and friends, do solemnly agree
That to whichever one success may come, —
Honor or Wealth, — the hand of Allah
    from,
This one to each companion dear shall make
Some worthy offering for Friendship's sake.

The years slipped by, and when good for-
    tune came,
It brought to Abdul honor, wealth, and
    fame :
Vizier the Sultan made him, and 't was then
He thought of Omar and Hassán again.

And they, 't is said, remembering the old
Agreement, came, their wishes to unfold.

First spoke Hassán : " Of thee, O Friend,
     my heart
Would crave of power to have some goodly
     part ! "
But Omar said to Abdul : " It were well
With me, O Friend, if I might ever dwell
Within the shadow of thy happiness,
And from Life's grape the wine of Wisdom
     press ! "

To each was granted that for which he
     prayed ;
The vow fulfilled, the promised debt was
     paid.
But soon Hassán, grown greedier, forgot
His love for Abdul, and began to plot
Against the Sultan and the kind Vizier
Whose hand had helped him to his high
     career ;
And at his bidding did a rascal's knife
Undo the thread of gracious Abdul's life.

Now Omar, he in peace and comfort sought
Wisdom, — a school-boy still, by Allah
    taught ;
Studied the course of planet and of star,
And for his Sultan made the Calendar ;
But most he loved, at the propitious time,
His gathered wisdom to record in rhyme.

To-day, of all these three 't is he alone
Whose name is honored and whose work
    is known.
Modest he was, and being modest, wise !
Therein the moral of his story lies.

THE CHRIST-MAS CAT

HE LOV-ED THE WOOL-LY CAT BECAUSE IT DIDN'T SCRATCH HIM WITH ITS CLAWS

THE CHRISTMAS CAT

It was the middle of the night
When Santa Claus, clad all in white,
Without a sign of any noise
Came down the chimney with his toys.
A host of pretty gifts he had
To make a little fellow glad —
Playthings of every kind and make
To please him when he should awake.
Among them, and the last of all,
A woolly kitten, fat and small,
He placed upon the moonlit floor
Close by the chamber's open door.
Then up the chimney quick he sped
And jumped into his snowy sled,
And hurried back with jingling bells
Unto the kingdom where he dwells.

No sooner had he gone away
When in came Mouser, grave and gray,
A sort of cat-folk *Santa Claws*,
Soft stepping on his velvet paws.

And there before his very eyes
The woolly kitten, half his size!
He bowed politely to his friend :
" A cat," thought he, "let that amend!"
Then pausing, with a puzzled look,
A survey of the stranger took, —
Saw that his eyes were open wide,
His tail curled neatly at his side,
His whiskers brushed, all smooth his fur, —
But could not catch his gentle purr.
So Mouser deemed it wise and best
To speak, and thus his friend addressed :
"Friend of my kindred Catfolk, here
Accept my welcome and good cheer.
I 've been a long time in this house
The sole destroyer of the mouse ;
Yet of the mice enough there be
To satisfy both you and me,
And you are welcome to your share
So long as there are mice to spare."

The woolly kitten silent sat,
Which much surprised the elder cat.
Then Mouser bade him tell his name,
How old he was and whence he came ;

And getting no response at all,
His hopes began to faint and fall;
Yet once again he spoke, his pride
Too great to let him be denied
Of courtesy and proper grace
By any member of his race.

"Are you," quoth Mouser, "such a cat
As would be thought aristocrat,
Too proud and prim to be polite?
To meet a fellow-cat at night
Halfway is what I wish to do,
But not an inch will venture you.
Know, sir, my lineage can tell
On mother's side, a Tortoise-shell,
And on my father's, if you please,
That ancient family — Maltese!
Our coat-of-arms is of the best;
A cat-o'-nine-tails is my crest!
Speak then, if you can boast of more,
I stand here ready to adore."

But never once the stranger stirred,
Nor answered Mouser with a word.
So all his friendship spurned at last,

Old Mouser from the chamber passed ;
With bosom filled with discontent,
And mood unhappy, out he went.
" I 've seen all sorts of cats," said he,
" And cats of every pedigree,
But until now I 've never come
Across a kitten deaf and dumb !
I pity him in this old house,
He 'll never hear a single mouse !"

.   .   .   .

But when the Christmas morning broke,
The little boy from dreams awoke,
And first of all his gifts was this
Strange cat who could n't purr or siss ;
He loved the woolly cat because
It did n't scratch him with its claws.